Thanks for being [a part of] my dream

PALOMA'S DREAM

THE TRUE STORY OF ONE GIRL'S MISSION TO HELP KIDS, INSPIRE ACTIVISM AND SURVIVE MIDDLE SCHOOL

BY PALOMA RAMBANA
WITH HILLARY RING

Paloma (signature)

Some names and details have been changed for the sake of privacy. The following is based on the author's personal recollection of her life. So far!

Acknowledgements

Thank you to collaborator Susan Joy Clark for her thorough research and detailed chronology of events.

Self Portrait by Paloma Rambana
Cover Art Design by Susan Boulo
Layout and Design by Cali Howerton

2915 Kerry Forest Parkway 104
Tallahassee, FL 32309

Printed in the United States of America

First Printing, 2018

ISBN-13: 978-0- 692-11278- 6

For more information about purchasing copies of this book
visit palomasdream.org

Dedications

This book is dedicated to my friends Chari, Micah and Alex, my mentor Caroline, my teachers Miss Jennifer and Mrs. Barton, and my Nana.

To my mom and dad: I may not be perfect but thank you for loving me. You are the best parental units ever.

Lin-Manuel Miranda you are the American Dream.

Thanks to the humans who read this book.
You can make a difference no matter how tall you are.

Alone we can do so little. Together, we can do so much.

- Helen Keller

Contents

1

Snap, Clap, Fund the Gap

This story starts on the steps of the Florida capitol, more precisely on the steps of the old capitol. In Florida, we have two capitol buildings. The new capitol is a 22-story skyscraper that was built in the 1970s because we needed more room for our legislature. The style of the building represents a new, more modern Florida. The old capitol with its traditional dome and red and white striped awnings still stands; they just built the new building right behind it. It reminds me of the song we sing at Girl Scouts about making new friends but keeping the old.

"You help me, and I'll help you and together we will see it through."

As a kid growing up here in Tallahassee, the capitol buildings are familiar sights and part of our history. On this day, I became part of that history. I was at school doing regular fourth grade stuff until my mom came and checked me and my best friend out early. We climbed into my mom's car, and she drove us from our school nestled in the pine trees to the Department of Education building downtown. When we arrived, a crowd was already gathered, even though it was chilly for April, at least for Floridians. Anything colder than seventy degrees is cold for Floridians. People still came out to support me and my cause. I lead the crowd on a march to the front of the old capitol.

There were friends from school, teachers, and friends from Girl Scouts. We had some strangers join us as we walked, our procession was gathering moss. There was even coverage from our local news station. I walked in the front, and my teacher Miss Jennifer held my hand. My best friend, Chari, walked behind me. We chanted as we walked.

"Snap! Clap! Fund the Gap!"

In Florida, there was a gap in funding for kids age six to thirteen who are blind or visually impaired. There were not funds for these kids to receive supplemental services like orientation and mobility training through the state in their schools. I am one of those kids. I was born with a rare eye condition called Peters Anomaly. My vision is about 20/200 so I can be considered legally blind.

On this day, I was nine years old and in the gap. As we marched, we looked like a mass of yellow because so many of us were wearing matching yellow T-shirts designed for free by our neighbor, Susan. Our shirts had the slogan "Fund the Gap" on the front in the same style as the London Underground signs that are typically in blue and red. In London, the subway is called the Underground and at the stations there is an intercom voice that repeats "Mind the Gap" while passengers board and exit the trains. The phrase is a warning to keep people from getting stuck in the cracks.

When we got to the steps of the old capitol, my dad, who is a lawyer and comfortable speaking in public, introduced me. My speech was written on a piece of paper that almost flew away in the wind. I wrestled with the paper and tried to secure the microphone. Miss Jennifer grabbed the microphone just in time and held it for me. I never looked up from my notes.

"Hi. I'm Paloma. Thank you for walking with me and all of the kids who are blind and visually impaired. Today's march is just one step to getting the state funding for my age group. As Helen Keller once said, "Alone, we can do so little. Together, we can do so much." Together, let's contact our lawmakers from my website, palomasdream.org, so the dream that 340 families can come true so that sight-impaired kids like me can be successful in their classes and their communities."

2

Phenomenon

I was my parents' first child, and I do not remember much about when I was a baby, but my mom has told me stories. Everything seemed normal when I was born, and we were ready to go home from the hospital. My dad had to go out into the parking lot to get our car so that I could be loaded into my car seat. My mom was left in the lobby in a wheelchair holding her new baby girl. While we were waiting for him, my body started to twitch in my mom's arms. My mom called out to a nurse on duty and by the time my dad got back to us, my pediatrician had withdrawn our discharge.

Mom and Dad waited five hours for a neurologist to see me. The people at the hospital thought maybe there was something wrong with my nervous system, such as epilepsy, because that can cause twitching so that is why I needed to see a neurologist. He didn't find anything wrong with my nervous system, but he noticed something else, "Has anyone noticed her eyes?" My parents had always heard babies' eyes were greyish white so they didn't realize something was wrong.

Later that day I was seen by an ophthalmologist and diagnosed with Peters Anomaly, a disorder that happens in about three of every 100,000 people. My parents got a second opinion from another eye doctor that same day. He told them the same thing: Peters Anomaly. Because Peters is so rare, the doctors started emailing other doctors about my case. Both doctors said I needed to have a corneal transplant in both eyes within about two weeks or there was a risk that I could go blind. The cornea is the clear front parts of the eyes, like the windshield. It is the most commonly transplanted tissue but if the surgery doesn't go well, then the result can be bad.

My parents wanted to take me to the Bascom Palmer Eye Institute in Miami, which is the top eye hospital in the country. At the time, South Florida was under a Hurricane watch because of approaching Hurricane Rita, so Bascom Palmer was closed. This was my first hurricane and like most hurricanes, it mainly involved a lot of waiting. Sometimes people have to wait in line at grocery stores, at gas pumps, or on highways, but in the best-case scenarios after the storm blows through nobody is left in the dark.

When Bascom reopened we got an emergency appointment three days later.

When we got there, we were told that the expert we were there to see, Dr. Eduardo Alfonso, was out of the office. We were shuffled down a hallway when Dr. Elizabeth Hodapp walked by and asked about the cute baby. My parents told her all about me. She said she had read some of the emails from the Tallahassee doctors and had already heard about me. She pulled out her cell phone and Dr. Alfonso was on his way.

Soon, three doctors, Alfonso, Hodapp and Dr. Craig McKeown, my Dream Team, examined me. Instead of risky cornea transplants, the doctors decided to create new pupils surgically so that light could enter my eyes and keep the optic nerve from wasting away. This surgery is called an iridectomy. I have also had another surgery to have my eyes straightened. I may have to get more surgeries in the future. When I am asked to read from the eye chart poster with the letters in decreasing sizes, the only part that is clear to me is the giant E at the top. The rest is a blur. The way I see my world has been described as seeing through frosted glass.

The first surgery I remember was when I was five years old. The nurse asked me if I wanted bubblegum or mint for the anesthesia mask, and I chose bubblegum. When I went to the dentist I always picked mint for anything that I had to taste but this was different. Actually, I did not know what anesthesia meant. To me it sounded like Anastasia, who is one of the stepsisters from Cinderella. I certainly did not know what it would mean to be under Anastasia, but I thought it would be better with bubblegum than mint. When I woke up, I was curled up like a cinnamon roll and covered in towels.

When my mom looks back at this time, she feels my twitch was God's way of drawing attention to my eyes. If we had just gone home from the hospital, I may not have been diagnosed in time. From my first day on this planet, I was already a natural at alerting those around me to potential problems.

3

Rasta Pastas

My parents met when they were attending law school at Nova Southeastern in Fort Lauderdale. They moved to Tallahassee before my younger sister, Belén, and I were born and opened a law firm here in the state capital. My dad is originally from Jamaica. When he was a little boy his mother left him and his sisters to come to America. She would tell him, "Better Must Come." My dad missed his mom while they were separated, but eventually she found work in South Florida and sent for him and his sisters. He left Jamaica. Better was on its way.

When I was eight-years old we all went to Jamaica for spring break. We stayed at a hotel that was like a colony of treehouses, each nestled into the jungle. A guide named Boxer took us out on a small speedboat. We motored through the clear water that was so transparent it felt as if the boat was suspended in air. Boxer slowed the boat, reached his hand into the water, and pulled out a starfish as large as my head. When he handed me the starfish, I could immediately feel it begin to harden in the air. The five arms were covered in nubby bumps. Boxer said it was a sea star.

"It's a starfish," I said feeling the weight of the displaced animal in my hands. We put the sea star, which is just a different name for starfish, back into the clear water and continued on our journey.

While we were in Jamaica we also visited my dad's father. Grandpa has passed away since we were there. His memory hardened in the Jamaican air.

My mother is Italian, so my sister and I have been given the nickname, Rasta pastas. Rastafari is a religion and a way of life originated in Jamaica and pasta is a big part of Italian culture, so that's how we got our nickname. We are a combination of our parents. My sister is three years younger than me, and she was not born with any disability, but I like to remind her that she will be driving me around one day.

When we were ten and seven, our parents sent us to an overnight Girl Scouts camp. My mom told me that she was worried we might be too young for overnight camp, but she wanted us to learn to take care of each other. When we are older, I might have to rely on Belén. The camp was in the North Florida wilderness on a lake, not too far away from Tallahassee, but it seemed like it was much farther away in time. A time before important technology, like air conditioning. When our parents sent us emails, they were printed out and delivered to us by giant snails. Or maybe it was just counselors.

We were assigned to stay in the green cabin with an army of other girls. It seemed that way to me at least. There was a cacophony of giggles and screams every night. I was on the top bunk, and it was so high that if I sat up too quickly I would hit my head. I lost a tooth while we were there, probably from banging my head on the ceiling too many times. My sister got pink eye. She woke up and her eyelashes were covered in gunk and stuck together. She had to put in eye drops for the rest of the time at camp, which was painful for her. I had my own opinions.

While at camp, we had to walk outside to another building to take showers, so I learned quickly about the importance of shower shoes. My sister and I had to work together to get the water to the right temperature. I was stronger but she could see the tiny C and H etched in the metal. We turned the knobs in large twists making it go from the temperature of melted snow to hot lava, causing us to jump and scream. Shower shoes are not just for protection against yucky floors but also for traction.

The best part of going to camp was shopping for all my camping loot before we left. I got a brand-new backpack and bug spray that was in the form of a bracelet. I even got a poncho that fit into a tiny bag, but the best thing was a portable reading light. It was my favorite camp supply. One night while lying in my bunk I was playing with my light, shining it up, and I could see what looked to me like bubble wrap packed in the corner between the wall and the ceiling. I was not an expert on cabin building materials, but I knew something was not right. When I showed it to my sister, she said, "I don't think that is bubble wrap."

It was actually hundreds of spider eggs. Right there above my bed. The Rasta pasta sisters, along with the other girls of the green cabin, were forced to evacuate. We had to lug all of our stuff on a long march across the camp to another cabin. After what seemed like the longest week of our lives, we finally made it home to the air-conditioned safety of our home with parents to take care of both of us.

4

Lighthouse

When I was only two months old, I started working with a special teacher named Miss Jennifer from an organization called Lighthouse of the Big Bend. That is what they sometimes call this part of Florida because it is the area where the shoreline of the state bends to the West. Some people call it the Florida armpit but obviously Big Bend sounds better. Miss Jennifer helped me get ready to start school by teaching me to use equipment like magnifiers to help me with reading and even a monocle, which is a one-eyed telescope like Mr. Peanut wears, to help with seeing far away.

Some of what Miss Jennifer taught me was called orientation and mobility training, so that I could go up and down playground steps and even learn things that some people may take for granted, like stepping up on curbs and not tripping. She taught me to make the most of touch, hearing, smell and the vision that I do have. We would work with Play-Doh, sand and other different textures. I also had to learn visual efficiency skills like scanning and being aware of color, size and contrast.

Miss Jennifer is a big fan of going to Disney World. I think that is why she is so good at her job working with kids, especially kids like me who need a little more imagination to get through the day. Walt Disney once said, "It's kind of fun to do the impossible." Miss Jennifer uses fun as a strategy, and when I was little I totally fell for it. She used stickers to make everything seem more fun. She would decorate my equipment, like my magnifiers and monocle with stickers. If it had stickers on it then it wasn't just a piece of equipment for the visually impaired, it was a piece of equipment decorated with stickers! Sometimes I was not so impressed.

My left eye is much stronger than my right so in order to make my right eye stronger, I used to have to wear a patch, just like a pirate. My girlhood dream did not ever include looking like a pirate, so I would hide my patches behind chairs and under my bed. It was a struggle for my mom to get me to wear them, but it was important to help me with my vision. Miss Jennifer brought her box of stickers and crafts to our house and suggested we decorate the patches. We covered one patch with sequins and then other ones we used the negative space and just drew streaks or stars. Miss Jennifer decorated one with a teddy bear making a heart shape with his paws. I remember sitting at the table rummaging through her craft box while my little sister played in the background. I forgot all about not wanting to wear the patches.

When I got older she would come to my school and teach me how to use devices, like Cecile, which is a big magnifier that has a screen like a television. I loved my first Cecile. I liked pushing the buttons and adjusting her cool color contrasts. When she eventually broke I was so sad because the company who made her had gone out of business.

Miss Jennifer and I are now more like friends, and she loves to tell me stories about when I was younger. She will tell me about how I used to go all over the place and get lost all the time. She also tells stories about going with me to my eye doctor appointments. She makes me laugh by telling me how I would cry for the whole car ride or even about how sometimes I just acted like an annoying little kid, and she could not wait to get out of the car. She likes to remind me that I wasn't always so cool.

5

Gadget Girl

$\mathcal{I}$ wear glasses, but I also have three other important gadgets to assist me with my vision. I have Cecile and then I have two other magnifiers that I named Lucille and ZoomZoom. Cecile comes from "CCTV". That's what it is, a closed-circuit television device that I can use as a video magnifier. After my first Cecile broke, my second one was not nearly as cool. It looked like an old-fashioned TV and only had black and white contrasts. Cecile also made a ghostly noise which drove me nuts.

Once I turned six, and I was in the gap, my family paid for my equipment and vision teachers themselves. I am lucky. I know that not all families with visually impaired children are able to afford expensive magnifiers like Cecile or other electronic devices to help kids in the classroom. About 80% of learning occurs through the eyes, so if kids who are blind or visually impaired do not have access to these devices to help them in school from age six to thirteen, then what will happen to them when they get to high school? It seems possible that for some of these kids they might have already fallen so far behind they won't be able to catch up. We let them fall through the cracks.

I have my third Cecile now. Since she weighs about as much as a six-year-old, I leave her at school and only take her home for summer. When I turn the power on, Cecile makes a beeping noise and the screen is so bright that it draws attention, which is completely embarrassing, but it has many special features like color contrast, super magnification, brightness controls, a photo option and zoom out, to name a few. I use Cecile mostly for math class. The struggle is real in math class, but I was inspired to do better in math after watching the movie Hidden Figures about Katherine Goble Johnson, an African American physicist and mathematician for NASA, who succeeded in her field during segregation.

I also have a MacBook, iPad and iPhone. These devices, even though they are not specifically designed for people with low vision, can do a lot of the same things that my electronic magnifiers can do. I am not always the best at keeping track of all my devices and remembering to charge them. Sometimes I will look at my phone and think that certainly 15% battery is enough, so I won't take the time to charge it. I try to be positive. Then my phone dies.

I have a few other old school magnifiers that don't have to be plugged in or recharged: some old bug's eye domed plastic magnifiers, and even an old-fashioned handheld magnifier that belonged to my late great grandfather. That one is very special to me.

At school, I use giant graph paper and other equipment like special "20/20" pens that write extra bold. I give my teachers jumbo dry erase markers to use so I can see their writing on the white boards at school. All these tools are expensive, though. Cecile costs about $3,000.00. The 20/20 pens are about $15.00 per pack and the dry erase markers are $4.00 each. Because most people cannot tell by looking at me that I have any vision issues, my parents always send a letter to my new teachers so that they will understand why I need to sit in the front, use special equipment, or take more time on tests.

I have also had to sit out from P.E. classes, too, like in first grade after my eye straightening surgery. I had to bring other activities to keep me busy during that time, so my mom bought me a fashion sticker book. The book had pages of dresses and other outfits, jewelry, purses, hats and shoes. More accessories than I knew existed. There were pages with girls, sort of like dolls, posing in different scenes. The stickers with all the clothes would peel on and off. My friend, Faith, sat out of P.E. with me and we played with the stickers together. I was happy to have company. Together we could do so much.

6

Race to the Moon

Ι sometimes have had to deal with disappointment because of my vision. It wasn't all giant magnifiers and sticker parties. When I was six, my parents signed my sister and I up for dance classes, and we would go to practices every week. When the time came for the recital, I was so excited. I was in my full costume with the flouncy skirt and knee socks with my usually untamed hair pulled back neatly. The recital was at a local high school, one of our historic high schools in a big red brick building that sits up on a hill in the middle of our city. The school has a real auditorium with a stage with heavy velvet curtains and wooden seats that fold up and down. Right before my group was going to perform, the dance director told me that I could not participate in the recital. He said that I might trip on stage or cause someone else to miss a cue. He said I could ruin the show. My sister still had to perform, so we couldn't just leave right away. I had to sit with my parents in the audience while my sister performed. That was a moment when I wish I could have been covered in stickers.

After that, I kind of gave up on dancing for some reason. I found new passions. My favorite classes in school are science and art. Those interests combine when I look up at the night sky. I have a collection of astronomy books that I like to read, and I have always been a fan of science kits. When I travel to the beach with my family, Belén and I will go out at night and use our telescope to look up at the stars and try to identify the constellations. On the coast we can see the stars better because there is not as much sky glow from city lights. I have even used my telescope at Disney World when we camped at Fort Wilderness. It was the same stars as everywhere else. That is one thing I guess even Disney can't make more magical.

Space really interests me, so I stayed up late one Saturday to watch the launch of the Atlas V rocket that carried a new weather satellite, the Geostationary Operational Environmental Satellites, Series R. or GOES-R. The rocket was launched from Cape Canaveral, Florida, the same place where Apollo 11 was launched in 1969 when it landed on the moon. I'm also fascinated that private passengers may soon be able to travel to the moon. Elon Musk, head of the private spaceflight company, SpaceX, is going to take civilian passengers on a tour around the moon. Mr. Musk is my idol and also the founder of Tesla, the electric car company that now even has self-driving models.

I was accepted to participate in SciGirls, a science camp through the National High Magnetic Field Laboratory— or MagLab for short—at Florida State University here in Tallahassee. The Mag Lab is the largest and highest powered magnetic lab in the world. It even holds sixteen current Guinness World Records for the amazing things the different magnets in the lab can do. Scientists come from across the world to do research at the Mag Lab, so I was excited to get to go to the camp. One of the days at SciGirls, we did a psychology test where we had to walk around the building wearing EEG (electroencephalogram) caps to track our stress responses. We had to do these little puzzles at a fast pace, which was stressful, especially while wearing caps with electrodes and wires poking out everywhere from our heads. The results were probably off the chart in the category of embarrassment.

I have also participated in a STEM (Science Technology Engineering Math) program through the MagLab where I was mentored by different scientists and learned about electromagnets and superconductivity. When I was a baby, the doctors told my parents that I probably would never be able to read or write, and reading was challenging for me at first, but with a little determination and the help of my magnifying gadgets, I learned. Technology has really helped me and has been a big part of my life, so maybe that is why I am such a fan of science or maybe I just like to think about how things work and how I can make them work even better.

One of my favorite books is The Island of the Blue Dolphin by Scott O'Dell, which is about a girl who is stranded on an island all alone and must learn how to adapt to survive. I also like the book Wonder. The main character is born with a facial deformity. He has had many surgeries, too. Sometimes he would hide his face in an astronaut helmet because he did not want people to stare or to see that he is different. Always be yourself, unless you can be an astronaut! Now that I am a tween, I have read The Fault in Our Stars by John Green, which taught me that there is joy—light—in even the darkest places. I also enjoy true life books written by activists and inspirational people like Helen Keller, my personal hero, who, even though she was deaf and blind, became a political activist, book author and lecturer. I like to read about unlikely heroes.

Another favorite book of mine is Kid President's Guide to Being Awesome by Robby Novack and Brad Montague. Kid President, aka Robby Novack, has osteogenesis imperfecta, a brittle bone disease that causes his bones to break easily. He decided to take that positively, and wrote a book on how to be positive when you're going through tough times. I'm all about positivity. Americans probably would not have landed on the moon if John F. Kennedy had not given his speech encouraging people to look at what human beings had been able to invent in such a short period of time. In his speech, he tried to explain what all our technological accomplishments would be like if we took 50,000 years and condensed them down to 50 years. He just used a proportion to demonstrate that we have accomplished a lot in a short period of time. At the end he said, "Space is there, and we're going to climb it." And we did.

7

Short for an Advocate

It all started with emails. Mom received an email from Miss Jennifer on March 9, 2015. At the time, the Lighthouse of the Big Bend wanted to advocate for school-aged kids who were not receiving supplemental services like orientation and mobility through the state. Miss Jennifer recommended that I go to the Florida capitol in Tallahassee to serve like a lobbyist for the Florida Association for Agencies Serving the Blind (FAASB) to "chat up lawmakers." She e-mailed my Mom, "Paloma is the perfect kid to help, because she is so articulate and well-versed in politics."

In reality, I was only a fourth grader just beginning to get involved with student council, but Miss Jennifer was being positive. It was like Kennedy's speech, "If Paloma's nine years were condensed to but half a year. The state capitol is here, and we're going to climb it!" Maybe that is a little dramatic, but on March 24, 2015, a Tuesday, I went to the capitol and had my first series of meetings with state legislators. Then I was asked to return, so I went back four more times, meeting individually with eight to ten legislators each visit. I was leaving my footprints on the capitol.

I dressed up and even brought a little brief case that I borrowed from my mom so that I would look official. I also brought one of my magnifiers to demonstrate how it works to some of the legislators. I created a presentation on my iPad to help me get my point across and to explain that there were 926 blind and visually impaired kids from age six to thirteen in Florida and that funding is needed for a children's program so organizations like Lighthouse can provide special training for those kids. This would include things like Braille training, abacus training, and training for listening, handwriting, orientation and mobility, assistive technology and independent living skills.

In Florida, our legislature has a Senate and a House of Representatives just like the Capitol in Washington, D.C. Actually, all the states, except Nebraska are set up this way with two houses. That would be a good one for Jeopardy, "The only U.S. State that does not have a bicameral legislature."

"What is Nebraska?"

The word lobby just means a group of people who are trying to influence legislators on an issue, like my issue of getting more funds to help the blind and visually impaired kids in Florida. There are lots of different types of lobbyists who represent all sorts of different causes. That day, I met with the chairmen of the Senate and House budget committees, Representative Dennis Baxley, a Republican, and Representative Alan Williams, a Democrat. Some lobbyists are talking to members of the Legislature about getting a new bill introduced or arguing against a bill that could eventually become a law. In my case, I was not trying to get a law passed, I was asking for what is called a Legislative Budget Request, hence the need for a briefcase. We were trying to get members of the Legislature to support having money in the state budget go towards a children's program to help kids in the gap.

Representative Baxley is a strong supporter of FAASB. He has a son who is visually impaired, so he understands and the issue is important to him. Representative Baxley is the chairman of the Congressional Vision Caucus in Florida and started the Vision Summit. This is an important meeting where groups can come together and talk about how to make things better for people in communities throughout Florida who are blind or visually impaired and even talk about how to prevent and treat eye disease. The Florida Vision Summit for that year had just taken place a month before I lobbied at the capitol. That might have helped my cause because at the

Summit they had a roundtable discussion, which just means a meeting where everyone at the table can get an equal chance to speak, about the gap in funding for kids.

While I was at the capitol, I was able to go into the House chamber, a large room with lots of dark wood from the paneling on the walls to the desks. Each representative has a desk that faces the front larger podium, so it is sort of like a big fancy classroom. Representative Williams let me pose at his House seat behind his name plaque holding his microphone. There is a portrait of each representative along the wall and a big picture of the Florida seal in the carpet at the front. The Florida seal has a picture of a Seminole Indian woman with flowers surrounded by Sabal Palm trees and a steam-powered ship in the background. It brings Florida's history together, like our old and new capitol buildings.

All of the representatives I met were nice and made me feel welcome. Some told me they were impressed that I was so young and already doing the work of a real lobbyist. Maybe not everyone knows that they can go and talk to legislators about issues that are important to them. I was lucky because I was working with FAASB, an organization who has people who carry real briefcases, but they need people like me who represent the citizens. I know from experience how important it is to get the services that so many blind and visually impaired kids in Florida were not getting. They need kids and moms and dads and teachers to speak out. We need briefcases and backpacks. And probably lots more stickers.

8

Challenge Accepted

A few days after I was at the capitol talking to members of the legislature, I met with Florida Governor Rick Scott and Lt. Governor Carlos Lopez-Cantera. My mom took a picture of me just outside the office, right under where the words "Governor" and "Lt. Governor" are embossed on the wall and then later I got my picture taken with the Governor. He even gave me one of his challenge coins. It is a coin that says Governor Rick Scott, Commander in Chief, with a picture of the State of Florida flag in the middle. I showed it to my class for show and tell.

That summer, Governor Scott signed the Florida budget which included $1.25 million to go into the children's program through the Division of Blind Services with $500,000 of that amount recurring every year, meaning that it was not just a one-time thing, that money would remain in the budget to help kids in Florida like me.

Of course, $1.25 million dollars was less than the $3 million we had asked for to fund a program for 340 kids. In fact, we really wanted even more, $8 million to fund the more than 900 blind and visually impaired kids in Florida. But this was still a success. My message had been heard. Funding in any amount for a children's program was better than what we'd had before: no program for supplemental services for kids my age. It felt even better because while the Governor approved our request, he also vetoed around $400 million in funding requests from different groups, which means that some people who were lobbying just like me, even the ones with real briefcases, did not get money for their causes.

A few days after Governor Scott signed the budget, my mom and I were guests on a local radio show called Tallahassee Talks. The host, Brien Sörne, has a voice that sounds like corduroy. It would be easy for him to write haiku because his syllables are so distinct he wouldn't even need to clap it out. Each time he said my name it started with a little puff.

My mom and I wore giant headphones and sat in his sound studio that had microphones on the wall. He used a MacBook as his main equipment and he let me play with some of the features. He wanted us to talk just like we were having a conversation. He introduced me, "Puh-a-Loma who has Puh-eeters An-ohm-maly." He introduced my mom and then summarized the work I did at the capitol. He made me feel flattered the way he talked about how it is not easy to do what I did. Then he asked me if everything he had just said in his introduction was right, as if he was gathering clues.

"Yes, that's correct," I said without elaborating.

He asked lots of questions to help me continue to tell my story, even though I think he already knew everything I had accomplished, but he wanted me to say it. He was just there to help me get it all out.

"How did that happen?"

"Did your mom help?"

"Then what happened next?"

"How did that go?"

"How does that feel for you?"

I told him all about my magnifiers, Cecile, Lucille, and ZoomZoom, and we talked about how they help me at school but are really expensive. I told him about the march and about meeting the governor. My mom chimed in to help add details. She used my experience as an example and told him that I could get a device like Cecile paid for by the state when I was five years old but because of the gap, not once I turned six. She used big words like *formative*.

He asked me if I thought kids with visual challenges ever felt discouraged.

"Yes," I said.

He then asked if the million dollars was enough and pointed out that we had only received a third of the funds we had requested.

"I'm going to keep going. We're not done," I said.

He asked me what I would say to help kids like me not feel sad, and eventually I got out the words, "We can do it!"

It is funny to hear my nine-year-old voice. Back then I still sounded a little wobbly, like Bambi as she tries to stand up on her own.

"Where do you go from here?" Mr. Brien asked and suggested – not too seriously – that I be a contestant in America's Got Talent or The Voice.

Mom answered, "We're thinking the White House."

9

Awards Season

Later that summer I was featured in a news story through our local public news station, WFSU. I was also named one of Lily's Heroes through KidsAreHeroes.org., a website that recognizes kids who are working to make the world a better place. I even received encouraging letters from Representatives, both Democrat and Republican, in the Florida legislature.

In September, right after I started the fifth grade, I was awarded the President's Recognition Award from the Democratic Women's Club of Florida. I was invited to a ceremony to receive a special plaque, and they asked me to give a speech. First, we all ate lunch. They sent a card in the mail for all the attendees to pick what they wanted to eat before arriving, sort of like going to a wedding. I had the chicken and it came with gravy and vegetables. Gwen

Graham also attended the lunch and at the time she was a member of Congress—the one in Washington. No pressure.

I was definitely nervous about giving my speech, especially in front of a group of people like these women who have probably been working for their own causes for longer than I have been born. In my speech, I thanked the club president, Dr. Maureen McKenna, for honoring me. I also asked the audience to join me for my second march on the capitol in December and also to contact the Appropriations Committee and their legislators through my website. Even more important, I was able to encourage them to get the "State of Vision" Florida license plate that funds support services for blind and visually impaired people in Florida of all ages. Getting this first award was an honor, and it made me feel proud, but it was also a big moment for me to go from speaking just about my cause of funding the gap to becoming an advocate for the blind and visually impaired.

After that I received even more awards, and I had to give many more speeches. I started to get more comfortable with each speech, looking up from my notes a little more, raising my head a little higher, getting a little more confident. In October, The Florida Association of Education and Rehabilitation (FAER) awarded me with the Government Leadership Award. It was the first time this award was given to a kid. There was a ceremony in Jacksonville in a large conference room at a hotel. My mother drove me the two and a half hour drive from Tallahassee to Jacksonville. I encouraged everyone there to join me in my second march on the capitol.

After the ceremony, we drove all the way back home even though I wanted to stay and eat at the Cheesecake Factory and then sleep in a hotel. I might have won a prestigious award, but I still had to climb in the backseat after a long day. With no cheesecake.

Next, I received the Paula Bailey Inspirational Community Member Award from Lighthouse of the Big Bend. That was also the first time this award had been given to a kid. I received the award at a Dining in the Dark event held at Florida State University. This is a dinner where all the guests eat a full meal in complete darkness. For this one meal, we could all experience what a totally blind person experiences every day.

This event is serious but also fun. The guests were blindfolded and given quick instructions on how to sit, walk and eat in the dark—like a crash course in mobility training. We went into an elevator and when we stepped out it was into a completely dark room. They even blacked out the windows. We were led to our tables and had to feel for the chair in front of us to make sure nobody else was seated there. There was a lot of "excuse me" being whispered. The Leon County Sheriff's Office SWAT Team was on duty with their night vision goggles to serve as our waiters. We ordered our meals from a card before arriving, just like the Democratic Women's Club lunch, but we still did not know what we were eating. The food was good if we could get it in our mouths.

Before we ate, the guests were taught to use a trailing technique, tapping fingers across the table to locate their forks and knives. Of course, once in the dark, there were a lot of people sticking their fingers in their sweet tea. As a kid, who has been reminded about table manners her whole life, I liked that all the other diners were unable to see me, even my parents. I chewed with my mouth open just to see what all the fuss was about. The jury is still out. I could tell that some people were nervous and some guests even had to leave because they could not handle it. Even for just one meal.

We sat in the dark for about an hour, eating or at least trying to eat. Then they turned on the lights when it was time for people to give speeches. I was asked to give a speech and so were both my parents. Through some tears, my mom talked about how important it was to provide services for kids in the gap so they did not need even more assistance, even more funds, once they turned 14. In my speech, I thanked Miss Jennifer for everything she's done to help me. I want all visually impaired kids to have someone like Miss Jennifer in their lives.

After that event, I published a letter to the editor in our local newspaper, the Tallahassee Democrat. I wanted to thank Lighthouse for my award, and, as an advocate for blind and visually impaired children, I wanted to raise awareness and encourage people to think about the unique needs kids like me have. I received recognition from many important people in our community, like our mayor, Andrew Gillum, who honored me with a proclamation during a City Commission meeting. My parents and my sister went with me to the meeting. Belén and I wore our yellow Fund the Gap T-shirts. The proclamation had a lot of "whereases" in it.

I also received a Certificate of Congressional Recognition from Senator Bill Nelson. Miss Jennifer and I went to Senator Nelson's office in downtown Tallahassee to receive the certificate. I even got a letter from the President, Barack Obama, who called me one of "tomorrow's leaders". Around then, it was sometimes hard to keep up with my other work, also known as fifth grade. My parents helped me to remember that being an advocate was important but there were other important things in my life to not forget about, like taking tests in math class and writing essays for language arts.

I had to remember that these awards were not just about me but for all the people like me that I could help by being an advocate. With each speech, I was like the voice on the intercom, "Mind the Gap." I was especially happy when I was asked to speak at a ceremony for White Cane Day at the capitol here in Tallahassee. The capitol, a place I used to just see out my parents' car window, was now a place where I was regularly doing important work.

White Cane Day is a national day in the United States to raise awareness about blindness and celebrate the independence and accomplishments of blind people. The white cane is an important tool of their independence. The white cane became a symbol for the blind about the same time that Ford sold more than a million cars, which was in the 1920s. Before there were a bunch of cars on the road it was probably not as dangerous for a blind person to cross the street with a black cane, but motorists were not able to see a black cane so easily, so they started using white canes which were more visible.

An important purpose of this day is to remind Florida drivers to watch out for people with a white cane. Our state law requires drivers to come to a complete stop when they see someone with a white cane or with a guide dog crossing or even attempting to cross the street. One blind woman spoke that day about how she has been hit three times by cars.

I don't use a white cane, but I understand how important the white cane is to a blind person's independence. I have an Independence badge from the Girl Scouts, and I related that badge to the symbol of the white cane in my speech. I was wearing my Girl Scout uniform as I spoke that day. Being in the Girl Scouts is important to me and wearing my uniform adorned with the badges I have earned makes me feel proud and gives me extra girl power.

10

Stay the Course

Fifth grade was not all about giving speeches and eating lunch with politicians. Like most kids, I like going on school trips. After lobbying, it is my second favorite way to get out of school. That year, I went with my class to Callaway Gardens in Pine Mountains, Georgia. It takes more than three hours to get to Pine Mountain, even though Tallahassee is only about twenty minutes from the Georgia state line. When most people think of Florida, they think of Miami and palm trees or Disney and waiting in lines, but Tallahassee is more about sweet tea and grits.

At Callaway Gardens, we did the Treetop Adventure, a big zipline and ropes course. My dad was with me on that trip, so he was able to do the course too. We had to go through a short training with a guide to learn about all the features of our harnesses and how to hook on and off from the series of cables that run along the course. I started out in life getting all sorts of training. I got physical and occupational therapy that taught me how to maneuver on the ground, so it made sense to get training on how to maneuver while five stories up a tree.

There are twenty-five obstacles on the course, things like crossing from one wooden platform around a tree and onto a shaky bridge. Most of the course was not that scary because even though it was high in the trees, a shaky bridge was still a bridge. At one point in the course, I was hanging above nothing or at least enough nothing to cause some real damage. At that point, I had to hook and unhook my harness, and I started to think about the likelihood that I could fall but then I pulled it together. The number one rule of ziplining is to not think about the odds. At the end of the course, I climbed a rope ladder up to a higher point, then sailed out 75 feet above the lake with a zzzzzeeeeeeeee. That was exhilarating.

A few times during the course I had to ask for help to clip or unclip from the lines or ask how to do a movement. I don't always like asking for help, but I don't want to miss out on fun opportunities or plummet from a treetop, so I have to ask myself, "Do I want to have a good time and try this or am I going to be embarrassed to ask a stranger for help?" I don't always choose to ask, but I did at Callaway, and I'm glad. There were two boys in front of me who were really confident at the beginning, as if they didn't need the training. They did not finish the course. They had to crawl down a ladder before the end. That made me even more proud that I finished the course, knowing that it is not easy. That was empowering.

I am proud how far I have come from needing help on the playground when I was little to completing a major zipline course like the one at Callaway Gardens. I did a smaller zipline before that day at the Tallahassee Museum, which is a funny name because it is more like a nature park, but that one ends with sailing out over the park café, so it is a little less intense.

That same year, I went with my family on a snow skiing trip to Jackson Hole, Wyoming. I was having fun at the ski lodge and on the gondola lift but then my dad dared me to try snow skiing.

"Double dare."

Next thing I knew I was clicking into my skis. I zipped up my jacket and pulled on my gloves. It was hard to fit my glasses under the ski helmet, but I got that on eventually too. The helmet was tinted, so it was difficult for me to see but that has never slowed me down before. I did lessons on some smaller slopes first, and they all had funny names like pizza slope. I guess that way kids would think it was fun and not just about propelling down a mountain on slippery sticks. Thankfully, I got through the ski adventure without hurting myself or anybody else. When we got to the bottom of the mountain, my mom was waiting for us. She stayed behind to sip some hot cocoa while we skied. She told me she was proud of me for trying skiing. Next time I might have to give her the double dare.

Being low vision hasn't really hindered me too much from taking on most activities. When my school started its first ever equestrian team, I was one of the first to sign up. I like animals, but I have never really considered myself a horse person. My sister joined the team, too. We rode at a farm not too far from our school and had a good but strict instructor, Miss Martha. Every session I would tack up, put on the horse's saddle and equipment and walk with the horse. I usually was paired with either Rio or Tahiti. After a while, I became more confident, and I was able to trot and canter. Horseback riding was good for me because it forced me to concentrate and be careful. It also helped me to learn to have good posture.

Miss Martha had very specific rules. For instance, we were not allowed to be in the grass with our horses and if we cracked our whips, then we would have to walk laps—as many steps as it took her to get to us determined the number of laps. She was strict because she wanted to us to learn. For me, she used neon-colored duct tape on the jumps and places where I needed to turn with my horse. She also cued me with her voice when to do certain things. I was able to compete in three horse shows, and I won ribbons, even getting a first-place ribbon at one show. I had to stop riding after Belén fell off a horse and broke her left arm. My parents decided it was a good time for both of us to explore other activities.

11

The Road Not Taken

Sometimes there are people, especially kids, who have been mean to me along the way. Having low vision can make me vulnerable to tricks. One summer during a day camp, I was running on a trail with a partner who I thought was my friend. I trusted her. As we ran, I could only see grass and trees ahead of us. There were two different entryways, one leading to a green area and the other leading to the road. I could not see the road because it was too far away. The green entryway seemed like the right way at first. My partner told me to keep going left, and I ended up by myself, out of breath and scared. At the end of the run, the girl told the counselor she did not know where I went. Then she laughed.

I wonder if any of the kids who have done mean things to me would want to trade places? I think about the grownups at the Dining in the Dark event who could not even finish one meal. Even though I do not look out into total darkness, I am not sure that everyone could handle looking out from my perspective. I am able to do a lot of activities, especially with the help of my family, but I am considered legally blind. I will probably not be able to drive a car when I turn sixteen, but I am optimistic about technology. I am looking to you, Tesla!

As if my low vision was not enough to make me seem different to some of the other kids, I stood out even more when I became a lobbyist at nine-years old. Maybe because of all the articles and awards, kids took that as a free pass to be unkind. Perhaps, they started to feel jealous and that was even more confusing. Maybe some of them would have, then, actually wanted to switch places. Whoa. It is like the upside down.

My mom told me that when I started to speak out about funding for blind and visually impaired kids in the gap, she thought other kids around me would join in and work with me for my cause, but that has not happened as much as we hoped. I try not to return meanness with more meanness and to stand up for myself and my friends. But I am human. I admit I have said mean things. I have also had people say mean things to me.

"You are pathetic."

I have also been called a loser, which doesn't seem accurate.

A girl called one of my friends, "a deformed weirdo" right to his face while I was standing there.

That made me upset, of course, and a little feisty. The next time when she approached us and said that he was stupid just like I was, I said, "He's not stupid like me, because I'm not, so get it right before you go ahead and just say it." I felt a surge of adrenaline after saying that, like I could lift an SUV off a baby.

I am in the drama club at my school and before one of our school plays, I overreacted to a comment from another kid, perhaps because people have been mean before, so I got defensive. Again, I am just a humanoid over here.

A girl passed my friend and me backstage and said, "Good luck." I thought she said it to be sarcastic.

"He doesn't need luck. He's got talent." It turns out she was being sincere, of course if she had said "break a leg" I would have known and simply said, "Thank you." I feel bad about that incident. My parents always tell me I should think before I speak and not be too sensitive.

12

Just Getting Started

Most of the time when I was meeting with legislators, attending events, or receiving awards it was during the week and during school hours, so I probably missed more school than most kids. Each time I needed to be absent my parents treated it as if I were an athlete doing team travel, like a kid who goes to regionals with her soccer team. The thought is that it will help me learn time management because I have to make up all the school work I miss on my own time.

I had a lot of absences that year because my lobbying work was getting a lot of publicity from local magazines and large national publications like The Huffington Post. The article in The Huffington Post was important because it informed people across the country about the gap in funding for Florida's blind and visually impaired children. The author also mentioned my website at the end so that we could reach even more people to help with the cause. The author wrote, "Paloma's campaign is just getting started." And he was right.

In November, I had the chance to speak at the 2015 American Legion Fall Conference General Assembly. By now, public speaking was getting easier for me. Performing in school plays probably helped build my confidence. Kids are a much tougher audience than grown-ups.

Just like on White Cane Day, I gave my speech the American Legion while dressed in my Girl Scout Junior uniform, sporting my green shoulder sash and crochet junior hairband. In my address, I told the war veterans in attendance that it was my goal to secure $6 million more to help the blind and visually impaired children in the funding gap. I talked to them about Peters Anomaly and the magnifiers and other equipment that I use that could help lots of other kids like me.

I even got a few laughs when I told them that when my friends at Lighthouse of the Big Bend asked me to go to the capitol to meet with legislators and then I found out I could get the day off from school, I jumped at the chance. Of course, now I know that doing lobbying work is not easy. Going from office to office and giving my presentation about the equipment and services for kids like me was bigger than any school project I have done. So far.

I urged people in the audience to contact their legislators

through my website and to join me in December at my second march on the capitol. During that same ceremony, the organization presented me with a medal on a red, white and blue ribbon and a framed certificate of appreciation.

My work to fund the gap was then featured in even more magazines. I was named "Amazing Kid of the Month" in Amazing Kids magazine, and an article in Everyday Power blog mentioned my lobbying success and recognition by the president. I was featured in People magazine, too. There was an article about my work in Tallahassee Family magazine, and I was featured on the cover. Being on the cover of a magazine was cool, especially in Tallahassee Family because we would see it around town, like sitting in the waiting room at the dentist office and there is my face on a magazine on the table. No big deal.

In the photo, I am dressed in a denim jacket and hairband, looking to the right, with my chin raised up and staring off into the distance. When my dad saw the photo, he said it reminded him of the famous photo of Jamaican musician Bob Marley where he has his chin raised up and is staring off into the distance. My dad liked the resemblance and that made me proud. Mr. Marley is also known for standing up for the rights of the people of Jamaica by speaking out and writing songs about social justice, which just means distributing resources more equally and treating people fairly. I have been listening to Bob Marley music since I was a baby. Maybe that is why I am not afraid to stand up for what I believe.

"Get up. Stand up. Don't give up the fight."

On the first of December, I had my second march on the capitol. We marched from the Department of Education building up the hill to the capitol. We all wore the yellow Fund the Gap T-shirts, and Mom and I made some matching Fund the Gap hair clips to give out. The hair clips had flat bows in blue and yellow and curls of narrow red ribbon. It is important to match your hair bows to your shirts. I am going to put that in my rule book about how to be an effective advocate. Maybe right after, don't forget to use the bathroom before the march. And dress in layers.

This time, I gave a slightly longer speech than I had the first time. I thanked my mom and Miss Jennifer and all my friends and family for their support. I also thanked Kim Foster the former executive director of FAASB and Director Robert Doyle of the Division of Blind Services. I explained what we had accomplished so far and then shared what we still needed: $6 million, to support all 1,000 tweens in Florida who are blind or visually impaired. Again, I urged everyone to contact their legislators and the Appropriations Committee.

Around this same time, I met with Florida legislators again. I had my photos taken that day with many of the representatives. I was back to working as a lobbyist. There are some lobbyists who do this work for their whole job and they get paid by companies or groups, but there are also lots of people out there like me who give their time to lobby for causes to help citizens in need. Influence Magazine recognized me as one of their White Hat lobbyists, which are people who lobby for important causes without pay. Maybe kids in my generation will be the ones to take back their capitols. Another good one for Jeopardy.

"What is democracy?"

On that visit, I brought copies of the Tallahassee Magazine to share with the legislators. The magazines were in a used Amazon box, but it accidentally was left behind in the cafeteria. Someone found it and called the Capitol Police because they thought there might be a bomb inside. My mom was out of town and got a call about it. After a few minutes of panic, they realized that instead of a bomb, there were just magazines inside. That is another rule of advocacy work. Never leave your packages unattended in a capitol building.

On December 12th, I had my second interview with Brien Sörne on Tallahassee Talks radio show. In my first appearance on the show, my mother helped me fill in the details about the importance of what we were doing and why this funding was so important to kids like me in Florida. This time, Mom did not speak, and I spoke with more confidence, even cracking a few jokes like an old pro. Last time I was on his show I was only nine.

After explaining about the funding gap, I told Mr. Brien and the radio audience, "So, here we are, in the dark, and everybody else is with 22 really lighted light bulbs, and we're like, 'Hello, can we have some of those, please?'" I said it dramatically, with a lot of emphasis on the "lo" in "Hello" and a lot of begging in the drawn out "please." I had him laughing. I was putting my training from drama club to good use, and I may not have known it at the time but I was really talking about social justice.

I was also awarded the Hasbro Community Action Award in New York City. I travelled with my family to New York to accept this award. I enjoyed meeting the other award winners, advocates from across the country with different backgrounds. While I was there, I got to see my photo on the eight story NASDAQ billboard in Times Square. We were told that my picture would be displayed briefly, but we did not know the exact time. We weaved through Times Square, with all the lights and everything already magnified, and made it in range of the billboard at the exact time to see my face on the screen. My mom was so proud that she sent a photo of it to practically everyone she knows. One of my relatives thought she had photo shopped my face on the billboard.

Since then I have continued to receive awards, such as

being named one of the top 10 Youth Volunteers in America by Prudential, and I have been featured in more magazine stories. I was even named a Health Hero by Oprah Winfrey for 2018. I received a letter from President Trump describing me as a "model of the American spirit." Two presidents and counting. I am proud of all my accomplishments. My parents have taught me that I should not accept awards or publicity as the reward at the end of all the hard work, even though sometimes I want to just eat a giant piece of cheesecake and crawl under the covers. Each time I am honored, I try to clip back in and set sail with a zzzzzeeeeeeeee!

13

The World Was Wide Enough

I have had to adapt to be able to do things that might be easy for people who do not have low vision, so it is nice when I get to go with my family to events that are adapted for people like me. One of my favorites is the annual beeping egg hunt at Pisgah Methodist Church just north of Tallahassee. The main church is a little white building built in 1858, and it looks like the kind of church you would read about in a classic novel.

They have several different Easter egg hunts and now that I am older, I usually do the traditional egg hunt with my sister, but when I was younger I would participate in a special egg hunt, where kids can search by ear for a beeping Easter egg. They pile the eggs together, or I guess the Easter Bunny does. If the eggs are in big groups they are easier to find. I had fun doing the hunt, but I remember being disappointed because the beeping eggs did not have candy in them. Their batteries take up too much room, but as a kid that was hard to understand. Once I learned how advocacy works with my Fund the Gap project, I have learned that I don't have to just accept things that are unfair, like not providing for kids from ages 6 to 13 who are blind and visually impaired or other important things like beeping Easter eggs that do not have candy in them. Through Girl Scouts, I am going to help Pisgah improve the beeping egg hunt so that more kids with visual and other impairments can participate with their families. And see if we can get candy in the eggs.

I have also played beeper kickball with both sighted and visually impaired friends at Lighthouse of the Big Bend. We were blindfolded so that we would all had the same vision, which was none. We had to rely on our ears to play. I have very good hearing because sometimes when one sense is weaker, the others can become stronger through better use. I can hear people when they whisper or someone will be listening to music really low or with their headphones on and I will say,

"Oh I know that song!"

"You could hear that?"

Sometimes I would overhear my parents talking when I was supposed to be sleeping. I remember one time they were talking about a gift they got me for Valentine's Day, so the next day I was not exactly surprised. Their sense of being able to communicate about surprises has probably become heightened now.

In beeping kick ball, we had to listen for the ball to figure out where it was and when to kick it. That could be tricky, because since we couldn't see where we were going, there was a lot of kid collisions. To make that game better, maybe we need to make all the kids beep.

I also like to read and write poetry. I competed in my county's Modern Language Expo and was invited to read poetry for a family services agency at Railroad Square, which is a funky art area in my town. There are warehouse type spaces and some have art studios or shops or coffee places. I read Langston Hughes' poem, "Harlem (What Happens to a Dream Deferred?)"

"Does it dry up? Like a raisin the sun?"

At my school, our drama club is called Junior Company. The big production for my sixth-grade year was a 1974 musical, Free To Be … You and Me. It is about how people should be able to be whoever they want, like that boys can play with dolls and girls can be bald. It is still pretty relevant. In other performances, I have played the part of Lucy in You're a Good Man, Charlie Brown, Tinkerbell in Hook and the part of Sarabi,

Simba's mother, in The Lion King. I have also played the part of Little Red Riding Hood. Acting has helped me to be a better public speaker.

I am a big fan of Broadway musicals, especially Hamilton. The playwright, Lin-Manuel Miranda, who also played the lead and title part of Alexander Hamilton in the original cast, is a genius. Even just the fact that people who might have fallen asleep in their high school history class, are singing along to hip hop songs about something like the Battle of Yorktown, probably qualifies him. Miranda also wrote In the Heights, which I also love. Many of the performers who worked with him on In the Heights have performed in Hamilton.

When I was in New York City with my mom, while she was there for a case, I was fortunate enough to see Hamilton on Broadway. My mom brought me some binocular type glasses to wear, but I did not want to wear them.

"Are you sure?"

"Yes, mom." Maybe, it was because I was a little embarrassed, but I told my mom that I did not need them. The set was simple, just a wooden stage with a balcony that ran along each of the three sides. There were not any big set changes or anything flashy. There were hardly even any props, just a desk or two and some chairs. In the center of the stage were two revolving circles that the performers glided and danced on. The audience didn't need 20/20 vision. Hamilton is all about the music. Even the choreography is somewhat simple. Except for at the end when Hamilton gets shot—spoiler alert!

At the end of the show, after the standing ovation, I asked my mom if the actors were black.

She gave me the you should have worn the glasses look.

I did not want to admit that I could not see the performers well, especially their complexions. Now that I think about it, maybe I experienced the show exactly as it was intended.

14

Yes, I Can

In the summer after fifth grade, before I started middle school, I was able to travel to Alexandria, Virginia right outside Washington, D.C., for the Council for Exceptional Children (CEC) Special Education Legislative Summit. The CEC had a mission for me and for my friend, Alex Campbell. We were both "Yes I Can!" Award recipients, which is an award given to students with exceptionalities who are doing great things. The CEC even set up appointments for me to go to the U.S. Capitol to meet with Florida Senator Marco Rubio and Representative Gwen Graham, who I met at the Democratic Women's Club of Florida luncheon. We go way back.

I was asked to advocate for the Cogswell-Macy Act. The bill, if passed into law, would benefit both deaf and blind students as well as deafblind students who have vision and hearing loss. It was named for Alice Cogswell, the deaf student who inspired Thomas Hopkins Gallaudet to start the American School for the Deaf, and for Anne Sullivan Macy, Helen Keller's teacher. The bill would require public schools to provide specialized instruction to blind and deaf students and would also help make expensive teaching and learning equipment, like magnifiers, more available.

I was excited and honored to be there for this cause. I was not even that nervous. The Capitol in Washington is not that much different from our capitol in Florida. It still has a dome, but it is way bigger and is always spelled with a capital C. It makes our old capitol seem cute. Not all state capitols have domes, and Florida might not still have one if they had decided to tear it down when they needed more space. The word dome helps me remember the difference between the words capitol, the building, and capital, the one that means everything else: the city, the money, an offense, a letter. A dome has an "O" in it, just like capitol. Now, I never get it wrong.

While I was in D.C., I toured the Capitol building and in the Emancipation Hall, I was able to see a statue of Helen Keller, one of my heroes. In this statue, she is still a little girl and is standing by a water pump. This was the moment when she first learned the word "water." Without being able to see or hear, it was hard for her to connect the words that her teacher spelled in her hand—this is a technique called finger spelling—with the things they represented. Helen was frustrated, so her teacher, Anne Sullivan, took her out to the water pump and spelled the word "water" as she ran water over her hand. She finally understood. By the end of that day she had learned thirty new words.

Helen Keller and Anne Sullivan are interred together at the National Cathedral in Washington. Without such an amazing teacher, Helen Keller might not have been able to learn words and be able to communicate and express herself. Perhaps, she would have always felt alone. Perhaps, she would not have become our most famous hero for the deaf and blind and deafblind community. Together, she and Anne Sullivan were able to do so much.

After sightseeing, I had work to do. I met with Senator Rubio in his office and showed him one of my magnifiers, my ZoomZoom device. Senator Rubio seemed very quiet and serious while I gave my pitch about the Cogswell-Macy Act, but he perked up when I showed him the ZoomZoom. He seemed impressed with all that it could do. A local news network in Tallahassee ran a story about our meeting. The comments section to that article taught me that adults can also be mean. I guess it is easy to say almost anything, even if it is an insult about kids, from safely behind a computer screen.

When I met with Representative Graham she said, "My office is your office. You're welcome any time."

I gave her a Fund the Gap pin and she put it into a glass case display with other pins. She also took me down to the chamber for the House of Representatives. The House chamber in Washington is much bigger than the one in Florida and the representatives don't all have desks. They sit in rows, sort of like at church. Also, there is a balcony around the top with more seats. I realized that this was the same room I had seen on TV earlier that year when my parents made me watch the State of the Union address. On this day, there were not nearly as many people and much less clapping. Representative Graham let me use her voting card to vote on two bills. I was able to push the buttons and put the card into the voting slot at the end of the aisle of seats. Then I got to see the vote show up on the Jumbotron.

During the Legislative Summit in Alexandria, I sat with my friend Alex on a Student Advocates panel. The two of us were able to talk about our issues in special education. Alex has autism, and he spoke out against the use of restraint and seclusion for children with special needs. He spent a lot of time as a first grader in the "crisis room," really a storage closet, as punishment for things like standing on a chair in class. He wrote a book about his experiences called Alex's Story.

15

Girl Scout Law

One day, my mom and I stopped for smoothies after school and were looking through the catalog of patches for Girl Scouts. We noticed there was a patch for Hearing Awareness but not for vision.

"Why don't we have one for vision awareness?" I asked.

"I don't know. Why don't we make one?"

And we did. We got in touch with Lighthouse of the Big Bend which worked with the Girl Scout Council of the Florida Panhandle. They designed a patch and created the steps a Girl Scout would have to complete to earn the patch. On April 23, 2016, the first group of Girl Scouts earned the Vision Awareness patch at an event in Tallahassee.

The best part of this experience, for me, was getting to work with other visually impaired girls, like my friend Kiersten, who has an eye condition called ocular albinism with nystagmus. This means she has reduced vision and that her eyes tend to dart around when she tries to stay focused. Kiersten has a wonderful attitude and outlook on life, and I really appreciate that about her. It was fun to work with her on this project.

To earn the patch, girls participate in an educational program to learn about various eye conditions and diseases. This program can be through their local Lighthouse or some other social service agency for the visually impaired. Girls will also learn understanding and how to politely communicate with someone who has a visual impairment. A third step is learning to be asighted guide for the blind.

The first Vision Awareness patch training and event in Tallahassee ended with a Dining in the Dark snack edition. Instead of a full meal, girls ate a snack while blindfolded to get a feel for what it would be like to be blind. This event was shorter but even more fun for me because my friends were able to participate and to get a feel for what life can be like for the visually impaired.

I was able to speak at other events, like Leadership Florida Connect, where I could continue to talk about fund the gap, but I could also explain about the new Vision Awareness patch and the steps to earn the patch. I even got to put my acting skills to the real test when I recorded a Public Service Announcement for Vision Awareness Month.

Then I found out about an upcoming Girl Scout trip to Europe, specifically England, France, and Switzerland. We would get to see lots of sights and do all sorts of activities. It would also be an opportunity for me to tell Girl Guides and Girl Scouts about the new Vision Awareness patch. I was going international. My parents said that I could go on the trip, but I would have to figure out how to raise the money to pay for it myself. I would not be able to use any of the money from Girl Scout cookie sales for this trip, so I decided that maybe even better than cookies, I could sell pies.

With the help of my family, I baked 24 pumpkin pies to sell at a fundraiser. I used my great-grandmother's special recipe for a pumpkin pie without a crust. I had my mother, father, and sister on an assembly line. The pies all came out perfect, but then when we tried to seal them up, the tops of the pies got stuck and looked messy. We were foiled! Well actually it was plastic wrap, but even though the pies did not look perfect, they were still delicious and helped raise money for our trip.

We had to have other fundraisers too. We did online auctions where businesses or friends give us stuff, like artwork, jewelry, or gift cards for all sorts of things and then people bid on them and the person who has the highest bid wins. Of course, it is not really winning a prize; it is winning the chance to purchase the item and help out the cause. We even had our local frozen yogurt shop, Nuberri, sponsor us by giving all their sales for one day to go towards funding our trip. We raised all the money I needed and because of that I enjoyed the trip even more.

16

Life is a Daring Adventure

The trip was in June after my sixth-grade year, and was just what every rising seventh grader needs, a nice long vacation. Our first stop was London where we got to see the famous Big Ben clock tower, St. Paul's Cathedral and the changing of the guard at Buckingham Palace. We also saw the Houses of Parliament, which do not have a dome by the way, but it is a bicameral system, meaning two houses, just like our government. Although maybe it is that ours is like theirs. We even took a tour of Windsor Castle where I saw Queen Mary's Dolls' House, a very elaborate dollhouse from the 1920s with electricity and running water and even—wait for it—flushing toilets.

Some of us were able to see the play The Braille Legacy, the story of Louis Braille, the man who invented the Braille system of reading and writing for the blind. The play was at the

Charing Cross Theatre, a small theater that is under Charing Cross station, part of the London Underground train system. While we were in London and in the Underground stations, I heard the intercom voice reminding passengers to "Mind the Gap."

In my head I added, "Snap, clap."

My friends and I got to meet the cast of the play afterwards, which was very exciting. I was able to tell them about Fund the Gap and other advocacy work. Some of them even tweeted about me, which made me feel super special, and even more importantly, they mentioned my website and Fund the Gap, which is great for my cause and all the people who I have been trying to help.

Then we were off to Paris, where I saw the Champs-Élysées, a famous Paris street full of fancy stores, Notre Dame Cathedral, and the Arc de Triomphe. We also went to the Louvre art museum. The buildings of the Louvre were originally part of a medieval castle. They have been updated throughout previous centuries, but they still look traditional and French. Then in the middle of the plaza at the main entrance to the museum, there is a large glass and steel pyramid that is completely different. It was part of an addition by the famous architect I.M. Pei. It reminded me of our state capitol buildings. Make new friends but keep the old.

The Louvre has more art than any sane person could see in a day, but probably the most famous item to see there is Leonardo da Vinci's Mona Lisa. I have actually seen this on a previous trip with my parents, and I remember when I saw it for the first time. I was a lot shorter then than I am now, and my dad put me up on his shoulders so that I could take a photo of it.

The Mona Lisa painting is so famous that most people have already seen it in books, in movies, on television or on the internet. I have even seen the Mona Lisa on t-shirts and magnets, coffee mugs, just about anything. When visitors to the Louvre see the real painting, it might seem different. They usually expect it to be larger. Most people trust their vision, so they are surprised when things are not as they expected. As I was looking at The Mona Lisa, a woman with a British accent came up behind me and asked, "Is this it?"

"What do you mean?"

"Is this all it is?" she asked.

Yes, this is all it is, just the actual Mona Lisa by Leonardo da Vinci. The museum was not particularly crowded, and someone told us it was because people can see art for free anytime of the day on the internet. I could get a Mona Lisa screensaver on my phone and see her odd smile a hundred times a day, but that is not the same. The internet can't show scale.

During this visit to the Louvre, Mom and I split off from the group and went to the Greek and Roman antiquities wing. I had recently taken an elective class on Greek mythology and knew a lot of Greek myths, so I gave my mom all sorts of information that I remembered from class as we were looking at the statues and other relics. The internet does not let you walk through the art with your mom.

After we left Paris, we went to our last destination, Switzerland. We stopped in Adelboden and stayed at Our Chalet World Centre, one of the centers for the World Association of Girl Guides and Girl Scouts. The chalet sits high up in the Swiss Mountains, and the views are like works of art. Helen Keller has a quote, "life is either a daring adventure or nothing at all." The Girl Scout Our Chalet in Switzerland is a great place to start an adventure. We had a Dining in the Dark snack edition while we were there, and I gave a speech about how dining in the dark shows people what it is like to live as a blind person, even if just for one meal or snack. It was there at Our Chalet in Adelboden, where I added the Vision Awareness patch to the giant patch board that took up a whole wall.

That was a big moment for me, and it all started thousands of miles, many time zones, and one big ocean away on the steps of the old capitol. What if when Lighthouse contacted us we had not agreed to speak out? What if my mom had said that we were too busy or that I needed to focus on school? What if I had said that I was too afraid? I did not have any expectations when I first advocated for kids in the gap. I did not expect all the recognition. I just wanted to help blind and visually impaired kids get the services I knew they needed. When I was a fourth grader standing on those steps, I did not realize how remarkable that was. I thought, is this all it is?

Yes, this is all it is, just my actual life, one adventure at a time.

Afterword

To my readers: Do kind deeds. Volunteer. Stand up for things you know are right. Try hard things. Keep trying and don't give up. Put your energy towards doing good things in school and in your community. Try new things and learn new skills. Ignore the haters and the bullies. You never know where life will take you. Always say yes to new adventures.

Thank you for reading my book. I would love to hear from you! You can email me at **fundpalomasdream@gmail.com** or post on social media using **#PalomasDream**.

Please visit my website **PalomasDream.org** where you can download my advocacy guide, connect with legislators, and learn more about my dream. You can also see lots more photos of my daily adventures!